Life's but a Poem

Peter King

This work is dedicated to people everywhere.

Preface
Life's but a poem

Life's but a poem
An epic to be sung
Of tragedy and luck
Of sorrow and of fun
But born we were
And die we will
While given for our fare
Life's sweet and bitter pill

Foreword

Christopher Hitchens is reported to have said
'Everyone has a book in them and that, in most cases,
is where it should stay.' And so I sat down to find out if
that be true.

An author now I want to be
And put down words for all to see
And by my works to all proclaim
The works I've written with my name

To sing of youth and all my dreams
Of adulthood and finding reams
To meet the challenges I'll face
And live my life at my own pace

And when in my declining years
I sit and laugh at all my fears
I'll wonder why I never did
Write down the thoughts I ever hid

But the task proved to be more challenging than I had
thought.

Here do I sit
My mind is split
The quill is bent
My clothes are rent

The empty paper's oh so wet,
the ink runs like a rivulet

and in my mind, the thoughts do fight
to find the words I want to write

'Tis dark in here
It's but a sphere
T'outside of which
I ought to switch

But then, I think I really ought
to clear my blocks with much more thought
Perhaps then, when the light arises,
My efforts will bring more surprises

However, there are physical issues that influence
completion of the task.

Now wearily, I lay my head
upon the pillow on my bed
And when the lamp is turned to dark
my mind alights with one more spark

A thought that is so pressing that
for morning's dawn, I cannot wait
But from the warmth and blankets cozy
I leap to write more words of poésie

And there is no guarantee of success.

Now my words I will put out
and get a printer to accept
With joyousness to noise about,
The excellence of my concept.

But now reality does bite
No printer is quite ready yet
To think my verses are quite right
So, I at home then start to fret

Critics on me then pour scorn
to leave me home and quite forlorn
But for their words I care no jot
And, so more verses do I plot

But not to be daunted, I carry on.

No Byron, Yates, or Shakespeare, I
My verse to heaven yet should fly,
To be there welcomed or rejected
I am by copyright protected

Should not the reader often feel
that verses to the soul should seal
The music in the written word
should freely fly like any bird

Though pundits and the expert's sniffle,
their opinions sound like piffle
For one man's taste is not for all
my verse the reader should enthrall

Prologue

If you're anxious for to shine
In the high aesthetic line
As a man of culture rare
You must get up all the germs
Of the transcendental terms
And plant them ev'rywhere
You must lie upon the daisies
And discourse in novel phrases
Of your complicated state of mind
The meaning doesn't matter
If it's only idle chatter
Of a transcendental kind

Patience, Gilbert, and Sullivan

Life's but a Poem

On Youth

Every epic needs a start

From out your caring womb I came
And with loud squeals I did proclaim,
I'm here to stay, so buckle up
My love for you will fill your cup

I learned to crawl upon the floor
but not to open wide the door
I waited till your hands were full
and reached your hem for it to pull

And as I slowly did progress
I also learned how best to dress
But in my room, left quite a mess
To which I never did confess

When often you did try your best
I studied how to do the rest
I quickly found when sent to bed,
you'd quit against a face bright red

Deciding how to play life's game
not in your home would I remain
I knew not much of life's swift pace
nor joys and tears I'd have to face

With loins gird up and brave of face
I swiftly ran to join the race
To see what's to be learned outside
And slowly moulding my own pride

I learned what other children do
As they moved quickly to and fro
But when I wanted to be fed,
I let my face still turn to red

Along with many other children, I had an imaginary friend

When I was young, I had a friend,
I sometimes thought lived round the bend
No other person knew he was there
and we together thought that's fair.

Together we would go and play
And act out scenes we'd never say
When I was sad, he'd make me laugh
and happy went we down life's path

But then, as I did older grow,
My parents and my friend did row
The final stroke that came one day
when I with him did join the fray

From then until the day I pass,
I'll rue my parents I did sass
But then he was my friend among
the many who so did me wrong

Then, one day, I started my formal education

Then studious did I become
to get a high degree
And not to join the common run,
from menial tasks then I'd be free

But little did I realise then
There'd come a day, I'd not know when
The work I'd done so furiously
Would not of ease me guarantee.

My earned papers I did hang
Upon a wall without a pang
Inside a room without a pane
And never to be used again

I wanted to achieve glory in sports

Great sportsmen have since ancient yore
been ready subjects of much lore
So, I, who's so much later here,
did hope one day to be their peer

Watchers all would shout their joy
as I my strength and skill employ
My limbs in harmony so move
Towards the line and medal trove

And when the race is lastly done,
I'd have the golden medal won
Spectators all would loudly roar
and many honours on me pour

But then a trainer tells me that
the efforts needed are not squat,
the joys I'll have to all forego,
if that's the path I want to go

Each sport, a special skill requires
To complement the spirit's fires
Looking not what others do,
but with much effort moving through

Each athlete comes prepared to win
And, by great feats make heads to spin
They strive to do their very best
and throw much further than the rest

Heeding not the burning leg
Nor lungs that for more air do beg
Dreading yet another step,
hoping to become sport's rep

But when of all the needs apprised
and basic efforts realised,
I had another serious think
And quickly stepped back from the brink

The beauty of sport

How worthy is it to perceive
what feats a human can achieve
To run, to jump, to leap, to throw,
to swim, and on still waters row

See how with both arms and legs
Before the assisting pole ejects,
an athlete can achieve full flight,
and thus attain a greater height

Watch as mighty arms do heave
discs and weights that hands do leave
and through the hindering airs do fly
to overcome what others try

When in a boat, an athlete sits,
and over water smoothly flits,
he checks the rolling of the slide
to easily on water glide

What e'er the sport they now are in,
the focus is on how to win
Looking not to see how far,
not letting dreams the efforts mar

Then one day one of Cupid's arrows hit me

Come, let me from young Cupid learn,
and for fulfilment always yearn
By labour and by love succeed
from any doubts be ever freed
For love should like some flower bloom
but never fade or grace a tomb

Da Li Shuang

Across the sea, you're far away
but in my heart, so near
But in my thoughts both night and day
there's none that is so dear

Love's doubts

Oh! Smile that lights my dark of day
Oh! Eyes that beam and show the way
Oh! Trunk that stands so tall and firm
Oh! Spirit that doth set the term
of many hopes and wildest dream
Must I my thoughts mistaken deem?

And when, though far, you are yet nigh
my thoughts across the distance fly
across the fields and forests wide,
across broad waters to your side
through darkened streets and lighted too
Ten thousand, thousand miles to rue

And, once arrived there now to rest
in your strong arms and on your breast
Your warmth and comfort now I feel,
my senses in mad dances reel
I hear your heart so strongly beat,
that all your hopes I want to meet

Oh! do not laugh and mock me so
lest from this life I forth must go
without the taste of loving care
And thus, unfinished, I need tear

myself away from near to you,
and never feel a love that's true

Why?

Who art thou to move me so?
Ask the ground lying low
Ask the rivers quick to flow
Ask the flowers which now grow
Ask me not, for I do not know

How do I feel about thee?
Ask the wind blowing free
Ask the leaf on shady tree
Ask the waves on shining sea
Ask the spirit deep in me

What makes you feel so right?
Ask the sun shining bright
Ask the stars with so much light
Ask the moon, a lovely sight
Ask my heart with all its might

Why to your side I want to fly?
Ask the birds flying so high
Ask the clouds up in the sky
Ask the dew on petal nigh
The answer is I need to try

Amor vincit omnia

Grumble, grumble, all is gloom
Early mornings warn of doom
Fearsome frowns adorn thy brow
And promise yet another row
All the past remembered is
Brought before and fully list
Yet once the joke is fully done,
Close thy lips and smile with fun

Smile, smile, and all is fair
no misery would dare
to cross thy face
or, find a place
in thy heart so pure

Deep inside, I really know
from your heart goodwill doth flow
A lucky man am I
to have you on my side
Love can really conquer all
and drive away the morning's pall

But love Is as fragile as a crystal

Love is a crystal, tall and fair
Graceful and slender,
so high in the air

Love is a crystal, pure and white
Its colours can vary
to give forth bright light

Love is a crystal, sound as a bell
music and movement,
its message doth tell

Love is a crystal, a wond'rous thing
to make music and magic
our souls raise to sing

Love is a crystal, alone so cold,
it needs another
for feelings to mould

Doubt is a hammer, cold and hard
Wielding much power,
makes crystal to shard

Doubt is a hammer, now in thy hand
a swing and a crash
on crystal to land

Don't swing the hammer,
Or is it too late?
Our crystal's too close
Let love tell our fate

Stop now, oh stop, oh stop

Our love's role

Enjoy the day and shed no sigh,
your loved one far is really nigh
Look out beyond what you can see
and feel the spirit that is me

All nature stands upright for you,
and I am there to help you too
To bless the earth with all your grace,
supported by your smiling face
Your love having passed the test,
provides a base where I can rest

See how the world replies
and how all nature strives to rise
See all the wonders that exist
to battle sorrows that persist
For love between us doth augment
the goodness of the firmament

On Maturity

The world around me

On Listening to the world

Is the world around you dark?
Only hearing mad dogs bark?
So listen, if you will, with care
And better in the night you'll fare

Hear the wolves cry to the moon,
and in the distance, hear a loon
A noisy trumpet you might fear
suggests an elephant is near
A lion's loud and mighty roar
is only there to scare a boar
Hearken to the monkey's screech
as nature reaches out to teach
you, not in solitary silence, sit
nor from the world around you flit

Listen then how others thrill
to sing and dance the days to fill,
with Fado or Gregorian Chants
to lullabies and choir descants
Listen how First Nations sing
to harmony with nature bring
Hear the mighty Zulus hymn
in praise of days that now are dim
Cry with the Celtic's various songs
that tell the world of many wrongs

As guzheng and bandura thrums,
hear the beating of so many drums
Harken to the erhu's wail

Compared to which the harp doth pale
Sense yet again the bagpipes' call
while pipes of Pan will never pall
Dance to bouzouki's stirring airs
and with Church organs, lift your prayers

That music is the food of love
the bards have told us is no puff
So do not revel in your gloom
inside your heart, for joy, there's room

On welcoming the new day

Apollo drives his chariot high
to drag the sun right through the sky
O'er mountains, rivers, and the seas
to warm the lives of birds and bees
To shine upon the blooms below,
and trees that stand all row on row

Awake, awake, the morning's here,
and for night's dreams shed not a tear
The sun and stars by gods were made
and, earth beneath was also laid
to which all creatures running came
The fit, the lazy, and the lame
sing praises and for blessings pray
and, hope the gods will not naysay

The seasons

The flowers that in Spring do bloom
dispel grey winter's passing gloom
And lead to summer's skies so blue
by which the harvests grow anew
And when the leaves show colours bright,
we know that autumn is in sight
And next, when snows begin to fall,
past joys we find we can recall

Flowers

See the flowers of many hues
showing whites and reds, and even blues
And yellows mixing with the greens,
to show how nature daily preens
Against earths blacks and darker browns
she watches you but not with frowns
The flowers with the sun project
a joy that you should not reject
To bathe you with a sense of peace,
and to the world your joy release

On the beauty of the world

By paint, and verse, and songs as well,
of nature's beauty people tell
The sun that lights both big and small,
the moon that shines o'er landscapes all

They wonder at the clouds aloft
and at the flowers of colours oft

they look around, and stop to smell,
and hear the sounds on air that dwell

They listen to the birds and bees
That sing and hum amongst the leas
They hear the whispers of the trees
so gently swaying in the breeze

They hear the many voices sing
as many feelings to them bring
And comfort and much joy they'll reap
as nightingales sing them to sleep

They watch the eagle soar so high,
the fawn that often comes quite nigh,
the fish that slumbers in the deep,
the ant that labours in its heap

They taste the many foods so grand,
cooked far away from where they stand
Like spices from the East join meat,
and sugars from the Isles make sweet

They hear the laughter see the smiles
though parted by so many miles
Happiness is all around
So why not let the joy abound?

Joy

    We, for our joy, do daily strive
    on lasting happiness to thrive
    And hear the laughs of children playing
    but not of pundits daily braying

To hear the sounds of harmony
but not those of cacophony
To see on baby's lips a smile
as kisses on it we do pile
To watch as couples closely hold
each other to in love enfold
To hear the sounds of wind and rain
that soothingly reduces pain
Help animals to come in trust
from outstretched hands to get a crust
To sit upon a shore and gaze
on nature's beauty and so praise
the bounteous world in which we live
and which to us much joy can give

Music

Oh list to all melodious tunes
That rouse or sooth a troubl'd soul
Hear sonorous tones the organ sounds
as to the heavens its music bounds
Fear bugles and trombones that play
To start a horrifying bloody fray
Hear too a stringéd viol produce
Sounds of joy or sorrow t'induce
But doth a dulcimer's soft plink
drive a harp player quick to drink?

Ballet

Let the music you entrance
as you watch the dancer's dance

Sit back and then enjoy your ride
by casting other thoughts aside
let your soul rise up on high
and with the rhythms go and fly
marvel at the artists' form
as the ballet they perform

Watch their toned bodies fit
the melodies of music's writ
As gracefully each limb creates
artistically fluid shapes
Next, they lightly cross the stage
How they can we cannot gauge
Now they leap a grand jété
that is certainly no play

For your enjoyment dancers train,
enduring sweat and often pain
By bringing value to their art
they help your troubles to depart

Painting and sculpture

The artist on a canvas pale,
wields a brush that's small and frail
It glides and blots with vivid paint
to thus produce a smiling saint

A maiden with a smile so coy,
beneath a tree sits with her toy
Inviting you to join her there,
to rest and picnic as a pair

Upon grey seas in storms that boil
join sailors who for safety toil
Or laze upon the ship's taffrail
to watch the sun turn night to pale
Gaze on blooms in gardens growing,
or in a farm a cock'rell crowing
And over hills and fields so green
a gorgeous sunset can be seen

From mighty trees or blocks of stone
are hewn a sculpture's mighty tone
These solids that stand very still
your cup of awe completely fill

Wanderlust

To travel farther, do you yearn?
Of Earth's great wonders more to learn?
To sleep beneath a canvas tent
Or are you more to lux'ry bent?
Does it matter where you lie,
If the view won't make you cry?

To gaze upon some tow'ring peaks
or sit by murmuring small creeks
Across great deserts wand'ring on
or for dark forests, do you long?
And make your spirits up to rise
to come across a great surprise

To view a flower or butterfly
and see much beauty by the by
Perhaps by waters oh so calm

your spirit seeks its pleasing balm
Then finally sit to select
the wonders on which to reflect

On travelling

Great journeys in the world we book
By train or plane or ship we're took
to see the sights there to be seen,
and visit where we've never been
Meet people who to us are nice,
and for our comfort sacrifice
Through fields and forests swiftly go,
across wide waters far below
Above great mountains that are high
and over plains we also fly
Past farms and cities do we speed
our memories for long to feed
And when at last we get back home
we then decide ne'er more to roam

People around us have different views

Do you accept a varied world
Or, has it to your views unfurled?
If with the world not satisfied,
Have you decided how it's fried?

Do my beliefs you trouble so?
Or can you listen and then let go?
Have I no right to go my way?
Or to you listen, I must stay?

If my skin's of diff'rent hue,
Should that distress one such as you?
Am I black or am I white?
Is that a reason for to fight?

What's my gender, you might ask.
Do you mind with whom you bask?
Am I gay or am I straight?
Must we discuss this in debate?

Do you believe the many lies
On which suppression now relies?
Such tactics really are not new,
but often practiced by the few

To make it better, do you strive
Or on much trouble do you thrive?
Can we together walk the talk
And from all efforts never balk?

On judging others

That man in God's image is
Created is our fav'rite bliss
And yet, we dare to query this
and seek to claim that He's amiss
We fail to see what He's created
but raise again what's long debated

What do we see when we look on
The man that stands the world upon?
Listen to his doleful song
telling us of so much wrong
Do we think we know what's right

But God's creation is a fright?
And fail to see the beauty there,
the grace and count'nance that's fair
See the sculptured torso glow
How the limbs with grace do flow
Is he tall or is he short?
Is his skin of some import?
Is his colour black or white?
Who are you to say what's right?
Do the eyes much joy impart?
Or do you only see no heart?
Can you hear his words of grace?
Or, in your mind, is there no space?

Hearken to the words of hope
describing beauty's wondrous scope
Hear his words of wisdom fly
from his mouth up to the sky
Warning faith ne'er to elope,
but with our works assist to cope

Pity me not

In God's image, so you say?
But look upon me, I you pray
See here, no arms or legs have I
No hands or feet for you to spy
Thus was I born of mother fair
But how can I with you compare?
Evade not your responsibility,
For pills, you gave t'infinity
Pity not what you see here,
but know, I lack what you hold dear

Oh Canada

Oh Canada, beloved home,
why did I leave the Earth to roam?
To seek the World's most wond'rous sights
When here exist such great delights

Where eagles fly across the sky
and circle mountains that are high
With hills that in their ice and snow
by rosy sun begin to glow
The cliffs of hues both black and brown
do over mighty plains look down

Hear in the distance Nation's drum
while nearby bees in flowers hum
See flowers that, in rains do bathe
and later, watch as ladies rave
Come see the trees rise to the mist
and hide what you should never miss

The beaver that has built its dam
in waters that for far did lam
Where salmon spawn in waters clear
oblivious of the bear quite near
Hear frogs that in green algae croak
and owls that in the darkness cloak
Watch moose and buffalo that cross
great highways for to feast on moss

Let's not forget the workers who
do toil and sweat in many a crew
on fertile land and forests dense,
to give us goods without pretense

And in the cities bustling so,
come over to enjoy the flow
of people who do work to sow
the seeds that in the future grow
to nourish and provide

Observations on the current world

Covid

Run, run, little bug!
in blood be quite snug
Joyfully and smug

Use your many ploys
treating them like toys
and scare all the boys

Spare no one at all
the short and the tall
Warrant all to fall

But be quite afraid
that Pharma's been paid
T'ensure you will fade

Lockdown Blues

As in lockdown, now I sit
my daily schedule have I split
Should I cook or should I drink?
It's too much trouble so to think

If to cook I should apply,
how much flour to make a pie?
Should a meat dish I prepare?
Or would a fish much better fare?

If to drink I now decide,
will I sacrifice my pride?

Fall to the floor in quite a state,
and let the neighbours contemplate

But then I think I need not choose,
but go to mix my foods and booze
With no emotions left to spare
the food can burn, I do not care

Mother natures is in a snit

Mother nature's quite annoyed
her anger is best to avoid
By wind and rain, by snow and hail,
by quakes, and floods that never fail
She throws men's buildings down a pit
to show them how she's in a snit
In face of that, what's there to do
But cry and start to build anew?

Urban living

Why do we love our urban sprawl
As through dense traffic we must crawl
Down streets that not intended are
For those who live without a car
Twixt buildings that block out the sun
and thereby rob us of our fun

The Metro and the buses flow
at speeds, we say, are far too slow
Arrogant and powerful too,
by day and night, they push right through

The taxis and the trucker's drive
as if last night they should arrive

The population is so dense
statistics now make no more sense
The crime is high, we live in fear
the police patrols are never near,
and yet, in spite of all of this:
Here is our happy home and bliss

Modern Housing

See how nature's green and pleasant land
to grey concrete is changed by hand
Great structures rise and reach to heaven
undying until that nine-eleven

The people that therein do dwell
in artificial heat do swell
And when the power has gone off
the living there gets really rough

Compare instead the lowly house,
with architecture to arouse
serenity and peace galore
Quite far removed from traffic's roar

Relax along with flowers and bees
beneath the cooling shade of trees
Enjoy an icy drink that's balm
within the walls of garden's calm

And pity not who lives on high

In housing that's up in the sky
Where nature's beauty is not seen
but stays as thoughts, what might have been

The chaos that surrounds me

As so much chaos I survey,
many thoughts come into play
How could so many nations fall?
How could my joys begin to pall?

The antics of the chosen few
my disbeliefs begin to cue
They bleat with much hypocrisy
to fool the people such as me.

They preen and prance as if with fame
when all that's theirs is outright shame
Entitled and so very vain
no traces of them should remain

But then a further look I take
and see my senses I mistake
I see the news although that's dry
informs me that I ought not cry

The winds of history come to blow
so disbeliefs and troubles go
The values of the pampered few
bring hubris for their future rue.

On modern leadership

Oh, ye who live near halls of power
and think yourselves to be superior
and with your peers, consider lower
those of rank so much inferior

Ye sacrifice the common people
Ye care not for their health
Ye think them worthless and quite feeble,
an only count your wealth

Of honour ye do nothing know
Not even to the law ye bow
Ye have no shame and no regret,
and faced with justice, you're upset

For nature care ye not one jot
but want to build a parking lot
Your many works pollute the air
for others' breaths ye do not care

From hist'ry's books, ye pick what's best
and to the landfill send the rest
Naïvely thinking which is which
ye easily do make a switch

Most civil talk ye do reject
but brays and guns ye do respect
With noisiness, ye seek to drown
the peace and quiet on which ye frown

Believing coloured skin Inferior
ye say your skin is quite superior

but truth be known, you're wrong again
by other cultures you're insane

Consider then that ye have shown
your views of self are overblown

Leaders take heed

Three sisters with a single eye
much coming misery descry
When reason is in short supply,
the sounds of evil multiply
When grace and goodness both do fail
together, strife and tears prevail
If leadership bows down to greed,
unlikely will the people feed
When fact and fairness are forsaken
heaven's mandate will be taken

Heed the voice

"À la lanterne." the people cried
and thereupon, officials died
Upheld no longer by the law
but so much fodder for the maw
of people who so long oppressed
their sense of justice did express
The lesson here that's to be learned:
The people's voice should not be spurned

America, June 2020

Great hills of granite to the skies aspire,
While you do linger by your fire
The warmth and light doth you seduce,
while gentle rains to sand reduce

For power and privilege have you yearned,
though history's lessons have not learned
Embraced hypocrisy and greed
to fill your yawning mouths with feed

Undo the measures of the past
for daring to disturb repast
Ignore the knocking on the door,
and throw good works upon the floor

The people's voice you failed to hear
For all your failures, now shed a tear
Lost happiness and safety mourn,
your voices be like winds forlorn

A politician and his fly with due reverence to Rudy

Pity the politician! But ask you why?
His great declamation attracted a fly!
For all the world there to see,
on his head, it had a spree!
How can he ever be respected
When by a fly's concerns deflected?
How ridiculous to sport a fly,
when trying to remain on high

Hidey, Hidey, Ho. With due reverence to a politician

Bunker, hunker, tickety bump
Beeping, tweeting, blustering lump
Nothing more than a clownish frump
He only thinks on us to dump
His leadership should us remind
he leaked secrets from behind
He's fractious, captious, but no mind
he's only there his teeth to grind

Wars

Surely, we should know by now
the world has suffered wars enow
But here we are with bloody swaths
as tyrants go down harmful paths.

No matter why they march again
Men and women both get slain
And if by deeds they do gain fame,
no one really wins that game

The aftermath is sad to see,
for wars leave only burnt-out lea
The young and old are left alone
for others' follies to atone

Dysfunction

The world's great nations are aflame
while leaders look for whom to blame
And whilst they look to solve the riddle,
Nero - like, they do but fiddle

That lives are lost, and lands destroyed,
means little to those not employed
in fighting horrors by the hour
but stay instead within their tower

Delinquents in abundance are
from sev'ral nations quite afar
They think that many deaths are fine
So, with their thoughts and prayers pine

But those who seek good deeds to do
are often stopped by very few
by those who enraptured are
to cause much trouble from afar

Still, others who to help would dare,
obstructed are in ways not fair
By those who don't give e'en a hoot,
and at the laws cock quite a snoot

The results are there for all to see
Nothing's done despite the plea
of those who come to voice protest
but are by forces laid to rest

Hypocrisy is rife

The world today is in a mess.
For why 'tis so, I must profess
that current use for currency
is only clear hypocrisy
The voice of reason is quite dead,
killed off by people who have led
their nation into fear and strife
By statements that are fully rife
with baseless facts and biased thought
T'ensure our loyalty is bought

See the man before you stand
with loaded rifle in his hand,
and loud proclaim so you will pause
to think that mercy is his cause
And also tell you to your face
it's not to do with people's race
Humanitarian reasons are
the causes why to go to war
This logic does not answer why,
but leaves us there to only cry

Don't turn away

With all the beauty in the world,
why is so much hate unfurled?
Can you afford to turn away?
Or why not come and stop the fray?

My dreams for joy and laughter

What is it that I'm after?
But joy and then much laughter!
To gambol in the flowers,
and bathe in nature's showers
To swim in lakes that are so cool,
and if no lake, then in a pool
On a river's verdant banks
sit down and rest my weary shanks
Then up I'll get and face the fray
to overcome the day-to-day

Survival

Survival isn't easy

The road leads on through hill and dale,
oft covered by dust and scoured by hail
Yet by its side a petal blooms,
and livens up the dreary trail,
to give us hope in life's travail

A river blocks my dusty way
to get across a price I'll pay
Yet in its deeps cool water flows
that 'suages thirst and dryness both
to give new life where life was loath

The mountain makes the road to turn
And too, the light of sun makes burn
Yet even then, cool winds do blow
to freshen body, thought and hope,
and from the hurt I soon can lope

On how to survive

The world has never been much fun
and to survive means: how to run
It also means we have to look
beyond what's written in a book

To face what lies ahead of us
requires that we have the nous
The obstacles and troubles will
not fade away to let us thrill

Thus, facing what's in our life's ruck
demands we have both will and pluck
So, we can think, or we can say,
or we can work, or we can play

Let's not forget we're not alone
or we'll regret when we atone
The choices that we make today
will let us rest or make us pay

On coping

All contradictions that in time
have led so many to be wrong
I will most gracefully decline,
and banish from my thoughts with song

To listen to melodious flow
and let my spirit float
down springs that to great rivers grow
and from the mobs, provide a moat

Instead, my object I'll achieve
with time and efforts dire
by following what I believe
But not what others do require

On being woke

Acting in a manner dumb
ignores where you are coming from
and if you don't know even that,
you knowing where you are, falls flat

If, for the past, you dearly yearn,
the role of change you still must learn
For nothing in the Universe
can make its onward course reverse

What in the past was good or bad
should not be judged by you today
You have those lives not lived a tad
so how can you say whom to pray?

Remember the past

Think what you have today
was built on blood and toil
of those who went before,
who each day tilled the soil

On Old Age

As old age arrives

Old age arrives without fanfare
before we're ready to accept
But now we for the end prepare
and must adopt a new concept

Spare no thoughts for all the dross
we gathered in our life before
Spare no time to mourn the loss
of vigour, friends, and so much more

Dwell not too long on harm we've done
but make amends if we still can
to those our friends who have not gone
but not to those who from us ran

Let's not regret the times misspent
for what is passed will ne'er come back
But to more joys our spirit's bend
of passing time, we'll keep no track

Let's marvel at what we achieved
and with our triumphs be well pleased
by helping others to succeed
in making their lives much more eased

Let's dress the way we never did
but always wanted so to look
We always wore what we were bid
but that's not written in a book

Let's do the things we've never done
and seek more ways to get new fun
Let's not sit there and be quite lazy
let's go out there and be crazy

Loss of values

From childhood, we were often taught
the values by which men swore
The crucial values so men thought
are love and trust, but there are more

Timeless as such values are
it's practice that rings true
But practise conjures ethics which
are followed by too few.

People who no ethics follow
can't live with us in harmony
Their acts we know to be hollow
and us will lead to infamy.

As Poohbah's of democracy
they preen across life's stage
Assuming meritocracy
in us, they conjure rage

An octogenarian man am I

An octogenarian man am I,
with memories in sev'ral patches
With limbs that now no longer ply,
and fashion that no longer matches

Through glass I watch the birds fly by,
and listen to the winds and rain
The sun and skies they fail to fry
my withered skin with joints of pain

My friends have gone and left me here
My children have forgotten me
And for my loss, I shed a tear,
and to the bathroom go to pee

Postscript

Weep not for me when I am gone,
For all my works, I will have done
And if these verses made you smile,
I'm happy you did like my style

The future's there for you, not me
But quail not in adversity
Go forth, face up, and be quite bold,
so that your story will be told

Disclaimer

Other than those public figures already in the news, no dead or alive person is represented in these poems.

Acknowledgements

I thank Elizabeth J Campbell, Lisa Arambula, Vanessa Dreme, Tina Giannoukos, Phil Logan, Lydia Montreuil, Richard Odey, Roger Shim, Li Shuang, Emily Lisa Thornton, for their inspirations, invaluable comments, and suggestions in helping me to complete this work.

About the Author

Peter King was born in Scotland and grew up in Switzerland and England before coming to Canada to study civil engineering at McGill University. He obtained his MBA at Western University and his doctorate from the University of Phoenix at age seventy. He spent his career as a naval officer, a public servant, a consultant to First Nations, and as a professor at the University of Hearst. For fifteen years he was a professor at the Beijing University of Technology. He has competed and coached in fencing, rowing, and cross-country skiing. He was also an international umpire refereeing at the world rowing championships. He has been recognized by federal, provincial, and municipal governments in Canada and by the City of Beijing in China. He has published two mystery novels. a history of rowing, several academic papers. This is his first poetry collection.

www.ingramcontent.com/pod-product-compliance
Lightning Source LLC
Chambersburg PA
CBHW070945120626
46546CB00004B/1578